Bilingual Edition

READING POWER

Edición Bilingüe

Record-Breaking Animals

The Stick Insect
World's Longest Insect

El insecto palo
El insecto más largo
del mundo

Joy Paige

The Rosen Publishing Group's
PowerKids Press™ & **Buenas Letras**™
New York

1

Published in 2003 by The Rosen Publishing Group, Inc.
29 East 21st Street, New York, NY 10010
Copyright © 2003 by The Rosen Publishing Group, Inc.

First Bilingual Edition 2003
First Edition in English 2002

Book Design: Michael DeLisio

Photo Credits: Cover, pp. 7a, 7b, 7c, 7d, 9, 13, 21 © Animals Animals; pp. 5, 11, 15, 17, 19 © National Geographic; p. 21a © Anthony Bannister; Gallo Images/Corbis; p. 21b, 21c, 21d © Indexstock

Paige, Joy
The Stick Insect: World's longest Insect/El insecto palo: El insecto más largo del mundo/Joy Paige ; traducción al español: Spanish Educational Publishing
p. cm. — (Record-Breaking Animals)
Includes bibliographical references and index.
ISBN 0-8239-6897-9 (lib. bdg.)
1. Stick Insect—Juvenile literature. [1. Stick Insect. 2. Insects. 3. Spanish Language Materials—Bilingual.] I. Title.

Printed in The United States of America

Contents

Contenido

Stick insects live all over the world. They like warm temperatures best.

———————————————

Los insectos palo viven en todo el mundo. Prefieren lugares cálidos.

5

There are more than 2,500 different kinds of stick insects. They all have long bodies.

Existen más de 2,500 tipos de insectos palo.
Todos tienen el cuerpo largo.

Most stick insects live on plants
or in trees.

La mayoría de los insectos palo
viven en las plantas
o en los árboles.

Stick insects hide by looking like parts of a plant. They look like branches or twigs.

Los insectos palo pueden esconderse fácilmente porque parecen partes de plantas. Se confunden con las ramitas.

11

Stick insects can hang from
branches. They can hang on
a branch all day.

Los insectos palo se cuelgan
de las ramas.
Pueden quedarse colgados
todo el día.

Stick insects do not move much during the day. Stick insects stay still so other animals will not know that they are there.

———————————

Los insectos palo no se mueven mucho durante el día.
Se quedan muy quietitos
para que los otros animales
no los vean.

15

Stick insects eat at night.
They eat the leaves on the
plants and the trees.

Los insectos palo comen
de noche.
Comen las hojas
de las plantas
y de los árboles.

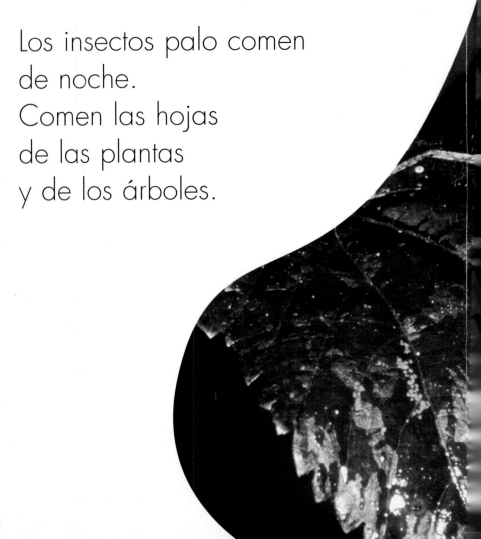

The longest stick insect ever seen was almost 22 inches (55.8cm) long.

El insecto palo más largo que se ha encontrado medía casi 22 pulgadas (55.8cm).

Stick insects are longer than any other insect. They are the longest insects in the world.

———————————

Los insectos palo son más largos que los demás insectos. Son los insectos más largos del mundo.

Cricket

Grillo

Cockroach

Cucaracha

Fly

Mosca

Ladybug

Mariquita

21

Glossary

branch (branch) the part that grows from a trunk or stem of a plant

hang (hang) to be held from above

insect (ihn-sehkt) small animals with six legs and no bones

twigs (twihgz) small branches or shoots on a tree

Glosario

colgarse suspenderse de algo

confundir no poder distinguir

insecto (el) animal pequeño que tiene seis patas y no tiene huesos

rama (la) parte que crece del tronco o tallo de una planta

Resources / Recursos

Here are more books to read about stick insects:
Otros libros que puedes leer sobre insectos palo:

Walkingsticks
by Patrick Merrick
The Child's World, Inc. (1997)

Walking Sticks
by Adele D. Richardson
Smart Apple Media (2000)

Web sites
Due to the changing nature of Internet links, PowerKids Press has developed an online list of Web sites related to the subject of this book. This site is updated regularly. Please use this link to access the list:

Sitios web
Debido a las constantes modificaciones en los sitios de Internet, PowerKids Press ha desarrollado una guía on-line de sitios relacionados al tema de este libro. Nuestro sitio web se actualiza constantemente. Por favor utiliza la siguiente dirección para consultar la lista:

http://www.buenasletraslinks.com/chl/tmb

Word count in English: 131
Número de palabras en español: 137

Index

Índice